th
boomslang

poems by
Joseph Nicks

this is boomslang

First Edition Copyright © 2020

All poems except those from 2019 have appeared in
previous MagPie books, often in a slightly different form.

ISBN 978-0-9971257-9-5

Published by Blue Jay Ink
Ojai, California
bluejayink.com

Book Design by Blue Jay Ink
Cover art by Ojai Digital

Credits:
page 11: © XYZ | Shutterstock
page 47: © Amy Schneider | Tower Drive, Ojai, 2017
page 79: © John Penezic | Dreamstime.com
Cover Photo: African boomslang Froemic | Dreamstime.com

This is MagPie Book #19.
Visit josephnicks.com for a complete list of
Magnesium Pie publications.

One-fourth of the proceeds from the sale of these
books is contributed to a fund that benefits the
following organizations:

The American Cetacean Society
Bat Conservation International
Black Mamba Anti-Poaching Unit
International Bird Rescue
Panthera.org

For Carla –

For Kirk –

For Kim –

*and their extensive past
and presence in my life –
anything I'd say of them
would scarcely do justice
to the durability of their
kinship*

*but I say it anyway
because it's all I have
to give them in return:*

*though they've probably
never realized it, they have
woven in and out of so
many of these passages*

1 gravicardia   *the deepening past*

3 dead reckoning   *the dissipating future*

Appendix A:

Appendix B:

gravicardia

the deepening past

*Though filtered through the rear-view mirror and
dust that's settled deep upon the seasons come and
gone, the past may be the realest of the three of time's
domains — if for no other reason than that it's already
happened. Further events may undo or undermine
those come before, but there's no negating history
(though the revisionists are constantly on the job,
generally trying to diminish what previously occurred
by dismissing or even destroying its evidence).*

*And memory is vastly underrated. Though those in
the know and the now so often try to call it into
question, or else endeavor to install their own artificial
implants (in keeping with their grand vision of a
humanity supplanted by an army of automatons), it is
that precious thing we cling to 'til the end. It is no
less than what defines us and if and when we lose it,
we descend into dementia, which is essentially the
loss of our ability to recognize ourselves, or place
those selves within the greater scheme of things.*

*The past is mostly steeped in sadness: The sorrow
and regret over events that have (or haven't) befallen
us, our kin, and kindred — or else the longing for those
seemingly happier times we probably no longer live in.*

Zenadirith

how is it that the wisdom
of these years so long and deep
and the layers of this
hoary outer crust
turn out to be
the youngest parts of you?

how is it all these answers
still supplanting all these answers
bring you back to the questions
you've been asking all your life?

how is it any altitude
your soaring heart may reach
sends it cascading
to the depths of you again?

how is it that the doings
of your uncontested prime
reverberate within to make you
whimper like a child?

how is it all this living's
brought you closer to your death?

could it be that all ascent
is an illusion?

Only For The Winter

bedamned but I still see it
though my eyes have long since turned
and cast their vision groundward
like an airplane's last low photographs
from just above the beachhead,
hanging frameless in the frigid halls of air:

alone not lonely figures
some kilometers apart,
unhuddled and unshiv'ring
but never far from fire

as the afternoon goes early
in the deepening of day,
these burnings lume into the lightlessness
so as not to seem so far away

but then it never grows quite dark enough
to obscure the icy distances between
lain down some long, lean years ago,
thinking it was only for the winter

eyes have frozen open,
not a tear can make the passage,
not a blink beats back the winds

only dreams are sleeping
and Earth is growing old...

A Number One Than Yesterday

do you know the bare of trees,
the frost of breath in air?
do you know the sling of salted slush,
the muffled crunch of footfalls on the shoulder?

do you know the Jesus Christ songs,
the peal of the distance in the bells?
do you know the moon of snowfields,
the stars of diamond cold?

do, you know – I do, you know;
not only that, I did;
did, you know – I did, you know;
before I even knew

do you know degrees of windchill,
the Christmasless, now-January winter?
do you know the shrouded silence,
the doorslam of the echo through the houses?

do you know the grey of skysteel,
the frozen flow of water down itself?
do you know the early sundown,
the pastel bleak of pink behind the trees?

do you know
the more you know,
the less you think you know?

do you know?
the more you know,
the less you think,
you know...

Vertebrates Of The United States

It was the 1957 edition, a John Glenn High School library copy I had become completely immersed in during those sophomoric days of Westland, MI.

Yep, there it was on that sunny afternoon in late January 1972, sailing smartly through the wintry air, pages fluttering helplessly as it passed from one big burly eleventh-grader to the next.

The rest of my books had already come to rest in the snow as the morbidly curious crowd began to gather in the field. As often as I pondered the point, I never came to figure out why it always took three bigger guys to beat the crap out of the skinniest kid in the school – and why no one ever intervened to lend a hand.

"Ha-ha, check this shit out – hey, Poindexter, what's a vertebrate?"

No sense in trying to answer, or even in trying too vigorously to intercept the hapless volume. It's not like they had any intention of dropping it until they'd sufficiently amused themselves. The book (and I) would fare better if I just acted as dorklessly as possible, kept my mouth shut, and endured a little shoving around. The sooner I was thoroughly humiliated, the sooner it would all be over.

The inevitable combination of kick in the shin and shove in the back sent me sprawling facedown in the stinging white powder, much to the delight of the not-so-innocent bystanders. Might as well just stay down. It looked as though the book was miraculously still intact and lying a few yards away, and that was the important thing.

A couple more swift kicks and a good solid smush-down of my head into the frozen sod and they were done. The onlookers reluctantly retreated, casting a few last smirking comments over their shoulders...

Well, that was adolescence. A few long-forgotten superficial scrapes. An equal number of deeply-festering inner wounds.

Ah, but we get over all that kid-stuff, right?

Right?

Ash Wednesday, A. D. 2002

four-thirty in the afternoon
in a warm and spacious room –
I'm spending some time
with my parents:

one sits waiting for the next friend
or relative to wander in

the other reclines peacefully
in a half-open box

outside the snow comes swirling,
ghost-dusting the black nakedness of trees

and I feel it now –
like never before,
the way she always said
it got into her joints

I watch her,
now so shiverless

and I resolve to never again
welcome fickle warmth of any kind

now that all my hope's been had

and so have I, for ever having *had* it

April, Come What May

the March was long and tortuous,
our ranks thinned by the day
and, April, green and foolish
with a thousand things to say
that blossomed into fever,
come what May –
we blessed each other
joyfully and sneezed:

again, again, a thousand times,
the tears run down our summered cheeks,
we danced upon the fields
and the fruit beneath our feet;
as ignorant as bliss,
unsorrowed as the dead
and dizzy as the water
down the drain

Lasting

when the moon
bathes our bedroom
in parallel lumes
enshadowed by
half-blinded panes,

when the breeze
feebly tingles
the left-behind chimes
of some ex-neighbor's
vacant backyard,

when dreams flicker
in porpoising consciousness
while memory flutters in vain,

I reach across the ages
time has gnawed out of our place
to plainly feel
the emptiness beside me –

longing for the distance
that will fade
this all to nothing more
than vague remembrances

East Or Sunday

weather-whipped,
wind-driven rain
ravages my roof
and rolled-up windows,
steamy with the breath of shallow sleep –
were you to wake me
and to ask me where I live,
well I could only say right here
and a thousand other places
on a thousand other nights

and I don't know from East or Sunday,
the 28th or Santa Fe;
where I am and why I am,
what time it is is all the same to me

but out across the framework
of a land as yet unscaped,
the hollow passages of lifetimes left unpracticed
thunder blindly in the distance and my ears

weather well enough or not,
I labor daily far beneath
a deep and godless sky
drifting in a more-or-less
north-yesterly direction,
I can't be lost if there's nowhere I have to be;
I can't be late if there's no one expecting me

and I don't know from East or Sunday,
the 17th or Manistique;
I don't know facts from figures,
the weather from the news;
I've no consensus, make no sense
of what my senses can't construe

but out across the hours
of sun-transected blazing blue,
I have lived my life in seconds of arc
and longed to tell the tale

weatherless, I wander
having lost my sense
of wonder long ago,
though murmurings still resonate
from somewhere deep down there

and I don't know from East or Sunday,
the chicken or the egg
or which came first or next,
already or not yet;
the date and my coordinates
are irrelevant to me,
the sand and snow and rocks and road
are all the same to me –
which way the wind scatters my ashes
will make no difference to me

but out across the roadmap
of the world emblazoned
squarely on my back,
I turn to realize I'm home
as I have seemed to me to be
a time or place or two before

Animals And Words

I looked up,
the sun looked down;
a good day for a ride
but the traffic wasn't mine
so I went back to work

I looked around,
the sky was there;
good day to write a poem
but the verse didn't stop
by here today
so I just wrote a check
to the water,
to the phone,
my landlord and the state

I took apart
a favorite song
to see why I liked it so much,
only to find I didn't
so I put it back together;
now it's fine

I woke up
the neighborhood;
good day to fall in love –
and I really wanted to,
but there weren't nothing
to fall in love with
so I picked up my wrenches,
walked downstairs to my garage

and in the late night radio,
I came to realize
that all that's left is words;
what's happened to all the animals
we used to pretend
not to be numbered among?

Pictures Of Life

in my eager younger days,
I paged through volume
after volume;
reading their descriptions,
examining their pictures,
immersing my imagination
in the stories
of the way each species lived

then out into the biosphere
I ventured with my mates –
at least the carved up remnants
that our suburbs would allow

in my squirming coming of age,
I drew closer in my pondered walks
from the museum to the zoo;
down the hallowed halls of intimate detail
and through the gardened air
to watch them breathe
and move around

then out into the biosphere
I ventured on my own –
straining at the canned preserves
that staved off premature extinction

in my mid-aged resignation
still unsettled by my weakening resolve,
I drove kilometric distances
across half-continents –
perhaps eight hundred hours
each eight-thousand-houred year
with barely glints remaining
of all the splendid life forms
I might yet cast my lonely eyes upon

then out into the biosphere
I ventured in recall –
beyond the disappointment
of the circumstance
surrounding waning life

in my faltering last decades,
I tap my reminiscences
like maple trees in winter –
remembering just how sapless
all these woods have really been

then out into the biosphere
I venture in regret –
for all the sacred places
of unvisited neglect;
I take out my would-be picture book,
imagining what life must still be like

Six Feet

I'm sure I'm not the first
to find a mere six feet of soil
to be of such unfathomable depth

but thirty-three years later
I still can't unremember
those fifteen

those near-sleepless sixty seasons
from summer '68 until the fall of '83
when all distance seemed to shrink
before our unrelenting run
through disillusioned days
and newfound nights alike

whatever hours we could steal
from the wicked lords of labor
and the slavery of study
we devoted to
our own fleet-footedness

and so we ran

for our lives
and what they might
turn out to be

somehow it slipped my notice
that our life-clocks spun
at different rates...

and up on Signal Hill
in the shovel-chuff of dirt
before the dawn
I committed him to memory
and I turned into the grey

to walk
no more to run
the long remaining years alone

where we once were six feet strong
now I find I'm four foot short

Simple

though I wouldn't trade this
for the simpleness
of those more simple-minded days
of breaking youth,
it really is
the simple things I miss:

like walking down this street
and simply walking down this street
without all the excess baggage
these years have obliged me to carry

like simply saying, "hey, good morning!"
and not having to stop and wonder
if it's true

like simply sitting down to eat
and contemplating nothing more
than chewing and swallowing
instead of all it took
to bring these things to my table

like simply lying here
in the still of the night –
in the depth of the night
and the breadth of the night
for the entire length of the night,
and not feeling so compelled
to try to reckon such
immeasurable dimensions

Who Would Want To Be The Last?

in some deep
and numberless hour
of some vague
and nameless night
so very near the end
of another anonymous bio
about to be tossed to the lost
and found

the barest of threads
dangle helplessly –
the fabric of a lifetime
come unraveled
by the passage
of acquaintances
and landmarks

flesh and blood
have finally come
to equilibrium
as some unknown soul
goes missing in the darkness

and in another lonely corner
of the same black monochrome
another someone wakes

to realize his life
has come to naught
though no ending's
yet in sight –
this same nothingness
will drag on
for some years now

Stolen Moments Of Gladness #3: *words and music*

OK, you win. I have to admit there is some scant
amount of happiness to be had. Right here among
the rubble of this sprawling anthropocentric
landscape; this trampled and castrated biosphere;
this digitally dumbed-down, over-automated,
selfie-posing cardboard cutout of humanity
and the vapid drone of voice-a-matic songsters.

But, fuck all that, and tell me –
is there anything in this world to compare to:

The way Alex Chilton growls *Gimme me a ticket for
an aeroplane...* just as you're sailing down that
work-bound onramp and cursing your miserable,
back-breaking blue-collar life?

The way The Drifters can take you *Up on the roof*
in those elusive rejuvenate hours that seem to be all
you'll ever be able to claim as your own in the
wake of another day's merciless beatings?

The way you can't help but join in with Bob as he
belts out that sneering, *How does it feeeel...?*

The way your eyes roll over until you can see the
back of your own skull when Bruce sings out
*For the ones who had a notion, a notion deep
inside, that it ain't no sin to be glad you're alive?*

The guitar solo that intervenes to shatter the
sleepless desperation of Chicago's "25 or 6 to 4"?

The way David Byrne reminds you *This ain't
no party; this ain't no disco; this ain't no fooling
around?*

The swirling transcendence of The Pretenders'
"Back On The Chain Gang"?

The mournful exhilaration and driving drone of
1980s-vintage R.E.M.?

Lee Dorsey's plaintive *Lord, I'm so tired; how
long can this go on?*, Sam Cooke's parched
Give me water; I'm thirsty; my, my work is so hard
or Otis Redding's beleaguered *I can't do what
ten people tell me to do?*

The oozing sarcasm of The Kinks' "Dedicated
Follower Of Fashion", "A Well-Respected Man"
or "Sunny Afternoon"?

The screaming disquietude of the guitars and John's
voice as "Revolution" bursts forth from whatever
speakers it just laid waste to?

The distilled disillusionment of Simon and Garfunkel
and their long, world-weary migration from swearing
that *I have no need of friendship; friendship causes
pain; it's laughter and it's loving I disdain* to
declaring *There were times when I was so lonesome
I took some comfort there...?*

Screw the sex and drugs, rock & roll is at its best
when it is living up to its *real* job as the poetry of the
people – the thinking, feeling, working, breathing
people.

Writhing Scientific

I. Coming Of Egg On Terminal Island

and when the season subsides
with only sand and feathers left
to blow through/against the fences

we sit down to take our tally –
yet another chapter
in the chronicles of
Sternula antillarum browni

the numbers tick off
so matter-of-factly:
three hundred four hopeful eggs lain down
in one hundred ninety-nine nests,
two hundred nineteen were hatches –
perhaps ten dozen or so survived
to leave the site with their fellows
by the seventh or eighth of August

that is, we know for sure
that thirty-three didn't –
and for four adults
there won't be another nesting

get past the feral felids,
the ingenious egg-gobbling corvids,
the chick, adult, and fledgling-snatching falcons
and your teeming, trampling twenty-thousand
larger cacophonous kin★

and you may live to learn to fly and fish
and lay down a few nests of your own,
perhaps a tern of twenty years or so

II. Post-Season Depression

it happens every summer –
no matter the close of a schoolyear
or the end of a nesting season

you watch the newly-fledged
so robustly come into their wings,
wish well so many others
still teetering uncertainly
on the fickly-shifting wind,
and bury your head in your hands
in heart-sinking realization
that so many never fly

III. Survivor's Guilt

between the fleeting by of decades
and the dragging on of days
comes the stillness of the hours left
to live in, take stock of your years

you hope against all hopelessness
you'll never wake to see the morning
you've outlived your
life-sustaining usefulness

and why I'm still alive's
a fucking mystery to me...

*Thalasseus elegans

At My Age

under the yoke of over

no once upon a time,
I've come unnumbered of the place
in these now-countless startings-over –
slate wiped clean
and words lain waste

but the dust
of lessons lingers
as a haze upon the board
and a few brave cursive strokes
survive the reach of the eraser
as if to silently lend echo
to the murmuring of memory
in otherwise empty chambers

Eight Mile Sigh

riding July by the window,
the moon on the highway ahead;
1983 or so and time was there to kill,
although I chose to spare it, just the same

the ride would soon be over
but no sooner than the night
and I drew a long, cool breath back there –
at least the longest, coolest one
the time and Tucumcari would allow

last night, the wheels rolled me;
I was taken aback by the seats
until the wind and longing road
rushing headlong past the bus
commenced the winnowing of innocence,
some years, now, overdue

and, with my shoulder to the landscape,
I exhaled long and deep,
let go at least
an eight mile sigh,
and gave away my sleep...

Time-And-A-Half

my dad had a back
that nothing could break –
not even 33 years at the plant;
the house is paid off now
he mows the lawn
and washes the car,
his back still intact
but something far deeper is broken:
all remembrance
of anything other than the work

my mom had a dream
that no one could touch –
as it turned out, not even her;
she still gets up early
and works in the garden,
which is hers alone
until everyone else wakes up
and invades her world;
what saves her is the simple fact
that she always knew
it was just a dream

I can't for the life of me figure out
what made them want to have kids...

Vangi's House

sitting here
on Vangi's doorstep,
waiting for what may
or may not be

the lights are going out now —
one after another,
but still I feel the flow
as it surges through her pipes
and still I hear the wind
rush through her curtains...

Whisperless

in the dead
of endless night;

in the still
of worlds devoid
of other inhabitants;

in the solitude
of shadows standing motionless
throughout an hourless land;

most any sound is music
to the silence –
most any word is news
to pen and page

Brontitude

southeastern Michigan in late summer

the distant flash of cracking sky
comes rumbling underneath
this greenly-wooded
rolling-meadowed land

you smell the coming of the rain
and hear the graveled wash
of rolling rubber passing by

you taste the twist of sorrow
in your own recumbent tongue

and through the toss and turn and tumble
of the leaves upon the wind
your eyes caress the ashen mantle
as it swiftly glides away

but all you *feel* now
is a deep and longing
thirstiness of heart
unquenchable as the history
that's been stealing past your home
in all the many years you've been away

The Burning Leaves

when summer's fat leans
toward the fall
and time and pulse
have quickened in the air;

when restless trees
are whispering
in urgency and eloquence
that knows no particular tongue;

when birds and sky
have gathered
for the distance,
I come home

and linger for a moment,
some two thousand miles away:
I'm not from around here
but I was

and now the burning leaves
enflame the trees
they've yet to take their leave of,
setting fire to the woods before they sleep

and now the burning leaves
me: emptiness, a withered hull
of undelivered goods,
my convictions acquitted all too soon…

You're Still The You Of Your Youth

even as the scores of seasons
pile up outside
while lofty dreams
still tower over
actual accomplishments

even as both girth and stature
radiate away
from younger heartwood

even though the losses
always seem to outnumber the wins
when you swore
from the beginning
you weren't playing

even though decay
has come to far-outstrip
all growth
and the dying is rapidly
overtaking the living

even as the yearning restlessness
gives way to not-so-quiet resignation

it's still you
so long, deep down there
at the bottom of your birthdays –
that youngest you has outlived
every later iteration
and it'll be that very last
glint in your eye
when everything else
you've been and done
may somehow
have fallen away

Down Fall

it's October
and I need to walk
because it's the only thing
I'm really any good at

though it's a stupid thing to say
because almost everyone can walk,
I mean to say I'm *really* good at it

in fact, if I might be so bold,
I'm probably one of the best walkers
in the world

and since autumn seems
to bring out the best in folks –
well, it's October
and I need to walk:

down along the gravel roads
and through their neighborhoods;
down upon the fallen leaves
and down into the woods

down beneath the bird-fled skies,
the copper, stony sun;
down among the flaming trees
and silver-frosted lawns

until these lingered, brooding weeks
relinquish to the winter all their colors –
until I find an alternate profession;
until I wake to crippled legs,
my feet are late for steppin'

and as westerly orange
is supplanted
by deepening indigo –
underscored by windows aglow
in scattered houses far below,
the hallowed moon ascends
to take its throne

I turn my collar into the wind
to catch the breath
of another year
before it sails

I set my feet upon the fields
and turn my thinking out
to do the thing that I do best –
it's October
and I need to walk...

cursive writing

the smoldering now

Of course, the only time that's ever happening is now
and it's the shortest kind of time you'll ever do – really
only existing in this instant. Most frustratingly
perhaps, it's the only time we can do anything about.
The past has been done – repeatedly. All we can
do is heed it as the only thing that arms us for the
present. And if we learned anything back there, it
will guide us as we usher the future through this
moment out the back door and into its annals.

The present is largely the domain of anger: Just this
minute at least it doesn't appear that it will do history
any favors. And the future? Well, we'll get to that
later (we hope).

You Are Here

in a place like this
you feel the cold before it's cold –
you turn to drink to keep you warm

in a place like this
you never listen to your heart –
there's not much left to think about
that anyone still cares to think about

in a place like this
we've traded our forests for orchards
our rivers for canals
we've converted our prairies to cropland
and replaced our thundering herds
with hamburger on the hoof

in a place like this
you lead a tertiary existence:
eight hours of every twenty-four
you work, another eight you sleep,
and the eight you have left over
are the ones you try to live in

in a place like this
the carrot jiggles enticingly –
the stick is getting longer by the day

and in the toll of distant timeworn bells
that mark each seventh dawn
what used to be our opiate
seems more like our placebo

Pard-on

I am not the lion
bellowing in the clearing
amongst his fellows
and his harem
as if to cower
all the savanna;

I am more the leopard
going silently and grudgingly
through the day and underbrush –
on his own
and on his way
back to the night;
the night from which
he emanates;
the night which
he eventually rejoins

Statistically Insignificant

neglecting air resistance,
I skated down the freeway
ignoring friction

assuming ideal conditions at STP,
I stopped to check my oil

it was 7 AM,
Eastern Standard Time —
we were lining up
for The Normal Distribution,
my best friend hung himself
with a rope of zero mass
and I could feel my own resistance
buckling underneath the toll of bell-
shaped curves

Just A Sky Away

rain, so fluid cold,
come down on streets and rooftops;
come gushing from the downspouts,
down to scrub the soapless alley cleaner still;
relentlessly come down
on buttressed tiers of untold stories,
anonymous pane upon pane

stolen looks through deep blue windows
in the swirling leaden skies;
windows rare and closing
on regretful afternoons

years blown clean and sober
as the chances of a lifetime
driven darkly through the middle of the day:

I smashed the phone today;
smashed it with one of my last remaining fists

now I just sit here staring
deep into its fractured ringlessness

and I smile in spite of the sky

Another Friday @ 1900

I stood by
my evening window
and watched
the turning tide

no the traffic's
never been a friend
of mine

sometimes I feel like
I'd like to remember
what it felt like
to feel like shit

but tell me
how can you remember
what you cannot
first forget?

Suburban Purpose

I live uptown
and I hate my life;
I eat my supper
and I fuck my wife;
I read my nothing-news,
subtract my ads;
I await my weather
and forescore my sports

I drive my car
down to buy some gas
so I can drive my car
to work to make some more –
more money I can use
to buy more gas

I go to school to learn
to change the world
into something similar
to what it is –
I store my data
and amass my facts;
I quote my figures
and collect my grades

I walk out of
the movie house –
I only hurt myself,
and going home right now
will only hurt somebody else
so I duck into some portside pub,
don't want to hurt no more –
I go to fucking Hell again
and slam the bloody door

gonna have me a kid,
gonna teach him shit
and he'll be bitter
because of it

gonna raise me a son
who can join the fight
and he'll grow up
to hate his life...

And None For The Days Of Not

a clean shirt,
freshly-laundered
of the aura I impart to it
as I labor long to earn my daily bread:
one for each day
of having to go out into the world
and none for the days of not

a smiling face,
unfurrowed
by the thinking it can't belie
as I ponder so much more than bread alone:
one for each day
of having to go out into the world
and none for the days of not

a lightened heart,
unburdened
by the beatings of a lifetime
and the yearning to at last be hungerless:
one for each day
of having to go out into the world
and none for the days of not

Midnight, Thirty-Eighth

step out into
the fog-enshrouded
silence of a suburb
sound asleep

not a single
dog is barking,
not a single
TV blares,
not a single
motor droning
down the distant
boulevard

and on this thirty-eighth
of April,
guess it's about time
to start calling
it May

but "May"
sounds too much
like a promise
far more likely
to end up
"May not"

Something #1

there's something in the morning
that incapacitates the night
and spills your life's forgetfulness
across the breakfast table

there's something in your pocket
that could help you change the world,
but for better or for worse
is what you can't know 'til you do

there's something about a junkyard
and the history it belies
beneath the gaping hoods,
behind the torn-out backseats,
time of death
spelled out in frozen digits
to the nearest tenth of a mile...

there's something in the basement
and I heard it late last night
but I would sooner go to Hell
than go down there to see
what I would doubtless see

Reptime

tomorrow I wake up
and kiss the morning
with a lifetime's-worth
of possibilities

tomorrow I take up
where I long ago left off;
take up the slack of sixty seasons
donated to a cause
without effect

tomorrow I wake up
to think on yesterday's crippled promise;
to ponder my former impotence;
to sigh with great relief to think
that that's all over now

tomorrow I wake up
but it's today

And In The Wake Of Sleep

how can I sleep
with the night
all around me like this?

and this something
these somethings –
squirming to get out
and into it again,
although they've never
really been

like a long, lean,
light-shunned shadow
cast upon the darkness
of the deepest, darkest night;

like blood spilled
inside my heart,
how could
anybody know
or tell the difference?

but still,
somehow I do...

how can I wake
with morning
smeared all over the place?

and that nothing –
those nothings –
come creeping in again
to smother me
and any dreaming I may have
forgotten to extinguish

like a sickly wash
of bile-hued paint
splashed all over the oozing,
pus-colored landscape;

like phlegm
on top of vomit,
how could today
possibly fuck up
what tens of thousands before it
already have?

but still,
somehow it does…

Drinkin' Michigan

I got the grass is greener blues
an' I been drinkin' Michigan;
a week, a day, another dozen months
until I set foot on this soil once again

I got airborne anyway,
my afterberth left trails in the sky

I got over the landscape
just in time to get back down;
I got down

I got no time for money,
got no money for The Times;
I got no need for newness
and no news is good to me

I got to get up every mornin'
'cept that last one;
I got so god-damned many ideas,
they're startin' to get ideas of their own,
and I'm only gonna be needin' this poor old back
about another twenty years...

I got the grass is greener blues
an' I been drinkin' Michigan –
I'm just about a million miles from drunk

No Matter The Mercury

when the winds have finally subsided,
having hewn the lifeless landscape down
to wood and sand and bone;

when the diamonds in the sky
connive to pierce the icy blackness
of the very air that freezes in your throat;

when not a single drop of water
is quick enough to trickle into
lean liquidity;

when the longest night of the waning year
is still 12 days away;

when the last of your inner heat
has escaped into the frozen atmosphere;

do you stiffen in your steps
as inertia and viscosity
creep into every tissue?

do you shiver in futile resistance
to the onslaught of the frost?

do you swear you still can't feel
what isn't there?

because the cold, as we all know,
is only an absolute and utter absence
of anything at all...

I Walk The World

I walk the world
in quasi-nausea,
unwilling to disgorge
the very things that poison me,
with the stubborn reasoning
that I'll finally wake one day
to find myself, despite myself, immune

I walk the world
in simmering resentment
of all that they
have forced me to become
just to grudgingly maintain
my marginal footing
in the slippery circumstance
of fleeting hominid advance

I walk the world
in slow-fermented guilt
for every cause I've failed to effect;
for every protest gone unlodged;
for each neglected chance
to punch them right between the eyes;
for every dozenth cheek
I've ever turned

I walk the world
in wonderment
of which I fear the most:
what they may, one day, do to me;
what I may, one day, do in turn to them

I walk the world
when wakedness wins, once again,
the war it's waged on sleep

most of all,
I walk the world
bent low beneath
the ponderous pall
of staggering, smothering sorrow
for every living thing
that's ever come unlived

This Shit

it's all right here for now –
this shit belongs to me:

my wind

my moon

you can't take them away from me
any more than I can take them away from you

and, until it goes away again –
until the wind dies down
and the moon is swallowed up
by the skyline of the city,
I've got hundreds of hectares to hike across
and thousands of thinkings to think

like how all this shit happened
and somehow continues to

like how I can't get up
on top of it all
and yet how I refuse to go down

like how, in any given bar on any given night,
you can stumble across those life-affirming things
in conversation with a stranger
or the way the music turns –
or you can shake your head to hear of things
that spell the *ends* of lives:

car meets motorcycle at 65 miles an hour

stalker meets ex-fiancée
out front of the latter's new apartment

two boys whose britches got too big for them
meet each other in the parking lot

but after you step outside again
and the night blows over you,
this shit just takes its place
in anything and everything out there...

...and the hours left to get some walking done

Slopeshot #99

up on the hill again today –
I went up there to take
another picture with my pen

it's smaller than the last time
which in turn was smaller
than the time before

that is, the hill itself's
the same size –
its viridescence is the only
thing that shrinks
until the tiniest of peaks
is all we working folk can get

the green of yester-vistas
that lent lung to
wounded spirit,
harried thoughtfulness,
and ache of day alike
has given way to
a different kind of green –
one man's reality
is another's realty

Eternitude

listen to how silently
these first stray beams
of freshly-broken dawn
have pierced the soft steel-grey
of the brooding harbor sky

watch again how gleamingly
they're cast across
the silver thalassic plateau
highlighting ship-peppered forever
lending shimmer to the sea

breathe deeply of how many times
some one or another among us
has paused to quench
both thirsty eye
and hungry heart at once

remember how unforgettable
each freeze-frame forged in flesh
and blood and bone once was –
as instantaneous awareness
disappears into the littleness of now

Under The Melanosphere

across the wide black ocean
I make eyefall
as wave on wave
of distant recollection
laps the jagged unseen shore
so many feet beneath my feet

where seasung birds sail headlong
through luminous wakefulness
all along this fleeting maritime of night

and I remember my life lessens
with every lunar phase
as I retread the sleepless gleaming
of hours that were never far from dark

Breverence

in a diner in the desert
on my way to where knows when,
the air feels painfully familiar
though I know I've never breathed
this breath before

seems as though it's been
the better part of forever
I have heaved against this earth
and my own mortality,
yearning mid-eternity
for just a little larger look
than the spark here in the darkness
of the eons gone unlit
and the ages
we assume are yet to come

another nanoscopic wake
in the ripples of infinity,
I know that I'll be dead

far longer than I ever was
alive

On Sadder Day Mournings

Mojave Desert musings #66

in the read-eyed wake
of faded flimsy promise
piling up on top of sadder days
too seasoned to be fooled
and yet still shoring up the weak
end of a quarter of a month

the cycling of the sun and
more importantly the moon,
the creeping planetation
of both mars and mercury,
cosmic jupiter-and-saturn's
far-away gigantitude –
all have lent their
pondered presence
to perturbing my inertia

and venus in the evening
helps me come into my own
to tap the world's nocturning
and drink deeply of the darkness
while it dominates the dome

but venus in the mourning
of another night's demise
can only bring me to my senses,
once again to realize

that if the dawn weren't prone to breaking
with such stubborn repetition,
there'd really be no need for evening –
there'd be nothing for the twilight to repair

Contemperature

within the heated traffic
of the stifling afternoon,
the future's getting smaller
by the day

though I pledge no allegiance
to the present that we give,
this time we trade away
to earn our keep

no I know just where the sun sets
before it sets anywhere else
and I'll be there to catch that
wherever still life breathes –
out where the night moves
only in its fourth dimension

because I've learned a thing or two
about the Earth, this age old orb
that contradicts itself at every turn
as west spins into east spins into west
and early becomes late enough
to somehow become early again

and back among the masses
where everyone simmers and stews
we reach for the midnight aspirin,
by now not half-expecting it
to take away the ache of generations

we wake up to the waning of the darkness
in the cold and stiffened daycreep of first light
and not one of us can help but be reminded
of just who and where we aren't

Field Trip

You want rattle?

You want hum?

You say you've got "no fear"?

No queasiness?

Come, take a walk with me:

I can show you darkness
you can't call the color of,
a thousand thousand miles beyond
"the night's Plutonian shore"

Where hunting's not a sport
and no hunter goes unhunted
for too long

I can take you down
in the machine-works
to watch the flesh and blood
greasing the wheels

I can take you out
to where the Earth
is skinned alive
and flyblown bodies
still crawling with life
and crying aloud
are buried prematurely

I can show you broken-minded
people who were born that way;
it didn't come from in-and-out-
of-rehab-whining "no! no! no!"

I can take you places that
negate the need for Hades –
where the twisted, tortured,
drawn-and-quartered
cadavers of humanity
will make you come unsuppered

And I can show you lingering
that curses life itself
and longs for greener fields
of restful peace
where we'll relinquish
all our liquids to The Styx

The End Of Almost Any Poem You'll Write

...but all those timbers
shoved so mightily
so many years ago
deep into death's
dark and gaping maw

you hear them cracking,
buckling now

you always knew
they'd only last so long...

dead reckoning

the dissipating future

The future hasn't happened yet. In fact, it never will.
It's the as-yet always imaginary realm of all our
hopes and aspirations, but we can never guarantee it
will behave to please the best of our intentions as it's
relentlessly devoured by the now.

It is generally with foreboding that we gaze into its
wide uncertainty. We may anticipate some fine things
yet to come, but one event we can't forget is our own
impending ending.

A Bullet For The Future

how many nerve-racked night times
will you lie there unasleep
with wave on wave of terror
crashing on the jagged shore
of your unsuperstitious heart

until you finally feel the urgency
of lifetimes left unlived:

hurtling down the highway
like a bullet for the future –
I can't stand another minute
in the presence of the present,
the clueless and cumbersome present
and all its crippling self-assurance

when you strip away
all the theatrics
and pare the message down
to ink and page,
the worth of any words
will come upon you, midnight-clear
if only your dry eyes are so inclined

and you may see the error
of your passive-fistic ways:

locked away in the chamber,
I've saved a bullet for the future
in bittersweet anticipation
of that restlessness–no–morn
when, having finally heard enough,
I get up the nerve at last
to shoot my mouth off

Chromonymous

there's a place
in the film
where everything goes black
and white,
stark-naked as the printing
on the page

and if you care
to read it,
it can show you things
no colors can obscure

there's a place
in the painting
where the water colors
everything it touches,
cleansing every hue
of its distinction

and commingling all
the pigments in its path:
sky to grass
and trees to sea;
bricks to fog
and flesh to soil –
though their shapes
may still define them,
I'd almost rather have
the thousand words

there's a place
within the music
where the words
have made their nests
and weave between refrains
with guerrilla clarity;
subjugated by musicianship,
I'd almost rather sing them
for myself

Movement 101

do the tracks lain down
upon the ground
dictate the gait
that laid them down?

is a river
more the water
than the way that water
wanders down to sea?

can the wind be still
and still be called the wind?

Far Things

somehere between
the depth of forever
and the wearing
away of days
another month is hung
on the horizon

sea and sky
so far con-fused
the blue goes on
to gobble up the blue

oh, how everythere
is magnified
by longing
and delirious
light-bending
atmosphere!

oh, how everyone
wants onelessly
to put their lonely pieces
to the whole!

oh, how long it takes
to learn how
to belong!

Parting

this morning I looked down
upon the stiffness
in the cedar shavings,
just an everyday occurrence

yesterday,
the day before,
and floating upside down
among the bubbles and filtration

one too many trips to my backyard
where they lie beneath the soil
and the chuffing of the shovel

is it any wonder,
after all these lives and deaths,
that some of us reluctantly
resolve to live alone?

Antarchitecture

to tell the truth, I lie
awake with certain women
on my mind;
not a one that wouldn't slap me
if she caught me
thinking of her quite that way

to plumb the depths, I rise
about a quarter of
the moon;
not a dream I care to entertain
if it means I'll have to
wake up one more time

to color life, I'll dye
my genes the fleshtones
of the dead;
no more than pigments
of their imagination,
so typically phenotypically
handed down

Tissues In Eternity

tissues in eternity –
formalin-addressed,
suspended sentience

the once-alive on ice,
gone now so germ-and-shiverless;
potential energy conserved

all the parts in situ,
trapped forever in their prime;
no furtherance, life history
to build upon that time

ageless perfect specimens
incapable of growth/degeneration,
metabolically inert,
perpetuated now *ad infinitum*

engines in antiquity,
now sparkless inexplicably
in spite of tireless dead reckonings
at roadsides, cages, mortuaries,
basements of museums:

poring over every pore
from sponge to *sapiens,*
bacillus to baleen;
expatriate biologists
exiled to the necrosphere –
in contemplation of the living,
we have walked among the dead
and grimly undertaken
such an inquest

do others wake these nights as I do,
frankensteinian futility enfevering their sleep?

Some Assumptions

you thought you'd just keep walking,
your resilient sense of sole
would persist and propel you
over any and all terrain

no destination distant enough
to be unreachable –
the march of time
would never overstep
your thirsty boots

but now, your legs gone leaden,
feel those sprawling green
expanses rolling back
upon the curling
of your map

you thought you'd just keep seeing,
that your eyes would always
penetrate the smoke and mirrors
of flimsy advertising,
the dark headlightless highway,
and the fine print
tucked so neatly underfont

but now, the blinding incandescence
of an unsated dynamo
usurps your weary vision
and swaps it for this cropped and
photoshop-enhanced illusion
of some fairy-taled future:
one hallucination under
Bill/Melinda God

you thought you'd just keep working,
that there'd never come a day
when you'd outlive your
life-sustaining usefulness

there would always be a reason
to rise up to face the morning
with your block-and-tackle back,
your flexion-steeled joints,
and the tools of a lifetime
still so firmly in your grasp

but now your plans have stiffened,
your resolve has rusted-fast,
the grease has gone to gruel
in your gears

you thought you'd just keep thinking,
never numbed by the negligence
of knowing nor unnerved
by the know-it-alls who
browbeat those who don't

skeptical of every easy answer,
unafraid of leaving questions
still unplugged for as long
as it may take to
fully quench them

but now your long-encumbered
reasoning unravels at the seams,
plagued as much by doubt
as mere dementia

you thought you'd just keep feeling
everything there was to feel,
all the pain and anger,
sorrow, apprehension
of what goes on within you
and without you

forever grappling with the phony joy
and sin-forgiven guiltlessness,
the suffering all around
of everyone who's worse off
yet than you

and now you know the only thing
you were always right about,
in the failing of your arms and legs,
your eyes and ears, your brain, your back,
your bladder and your bowels

one part of you remains
to take its beatings
and its bleeding
to the end

Dirt For Dessert

We'll give them
drive-thru
caffeinated hope
for breakfast,

a toke or two's
forgetfulness
for lunch,

half a dozen
shots of
drunken
distraction
for dinner,

a freshly-butchered
flesh-and-blood
last supper,

and when the smoke
and mirrors
of a lifetime clear,

they'll all have
dirt for dessert.

Groundless

on such a tree-tossed snatch of afternoon,
relieved of your dis-ease for a moment or so,
you pause upon the precipice –
your eyes skip out across October's ocean

but terrain-bound as your limbs are,
you realize you have no business there...

so you come back to looking back,
kilometers and days almost unnumbered
since your tried and tired boots were shaken
clean of native soil –
who's to say now
if it's what you should have done?

or not?

because in the interplay of wind and sun
and clear-as-yester ferrotypes of distant memory,
you feel it just as keenly
that you have no business *here*

and perhaps this yearning nowhereness
is as much your home as any-here has been

Sometimes I Lie So Wide

awake

and listen to the wind
wash across the desert shore
a rising tide
so easterly unebbing

and know that there's
another place
I should've been
and should be

sometimes I lie in deep
unsleep-

ing achedness and hope
counting all the thin
and hungered years
that slipped right through
the best of our intentions

and feel how few
are likely left
to finish what
we've started

sometimes I lie to anyone
who might be over hearing this
that someday soon
it's going to be OK

nobody's gonna suffer anymore

but tell it to that organ
that pounds up through my pillow
and bleeds into my dreams

and makes me wonder
in the dimlit hours
just how long
these beatings will continue

Full Cycle

yes to day
and no to morrow,
I was up on two wheels again,
rethinking my long-standing pacifism
and breathing in between the broken lines

the night belonged to my bike
and the throttle belonged to me,
I belonged to the road
and the road belonged to the night –
and a week and a day and a half later,
The Everglades still burned in my eyes...

and every now and then
I look around –
and find me in the now, and then
I know the wind

will blow full cycle
and then back around again
all along the longing road,
longing for the last of this
and lasting all night long

and, out here in the middle
of my gas tank and the night,

"it really can't get any darker, right?"
I ask nobody there

Before The Fall

though far more subtle here
than where I used to live,
with some years practice
you'll discern it just the same

that rare, impatient character
the autumn air assumes,
each afternoon gone sooner –
deeper gold,
as if ushered into evening
by the wind

and, though we have less
than the rest of September
to spirit the summer away,
there is a far and widened
calmness in the sky

as all the landscape grows October,
so stunningly-seasoned and sober,
you won't find a better time
for taking stock of all the colors
you once were and have become

The Earthen Autumnation

when the last ill lumens of the day
disappear on the Hesperian horizon
and trees have nothing left
to do but breathe and breathe
their secrets to the wind

I set out in the wake
of the workweek
and I say good bye to sleep

alone in my own
twilight zones, I tune
my ears to October –
in all its flux and
restless pre-quiescence

my pulse quickens
with uncertainty,
anticipating seasons
that I have no real reason
to expect I'll live to see

even as my gravid heart
descends into
the memory-laden past

I trudge the fallen browns
and reds and yellows,
as tired as the Earth
and yet as burning
as the color they still lend
the dusky landscape:

this is where you go
when yet another year
has gotten the better of you
and no corner of the world
remains unsorrowed

this is where you go
when it feels as if
you must be soon to go

this is where you go
when you find
you need to know
you're still alive

From Here To Uncertainty

the slowly
sky-crossed sun
seems to hint at
an unhurried
and eternal
turn of Earth

where we not only
have forever
but we can make
the same mistake
of not making anything
of this day
or the next day
or the next

whereas the wind
in all its swirling restlessness
whispers its reminders
that tomorrow
is a finite proposition

as uncertain
as today was
yesterday

In The Lateness Of The Day

I come home in autumn's
auburn afternoon

I drag myself inside
and bolt the door
and raise the blinds
and peer deep
into the creeping indigo
that separates the daytime
from the darkness

And as I lie here
with what's left of life
so bruised and slowly
oozing out of me,

I can plainly hear
the weeping agony –
the sorrow, fear, and anger
of most everything that lives

And I swear I just
can't take it anymore...

But in the morning,
come the sun, somehow
I rise and I go out there
to take it all some more

Just stupid, I guess...

November No More

it's October's after-equinox –
the ambered autumn air,
the coppery senescence
of the sun set sail for solstice
on the arc of Earth's illusion

it's the scarlet, sulfur
flaming of the forests
in farewell

it's the way you watch
so flightlessly
the wave on wave
of outward-bound
as they join the distant sky
and disappear

it's that hallowed when of whens
each year must funnel through
on its lonely way to winter
once again

it's all these things embodied
in the night of the living,
day of the dead –
anticipation come confused
with recollection
of life after life,
afterlife presupposed   .

and each new wind
that comes astir
of the now-denuded trees
blows a little colder
than the last

in the ache of all these seasons,
you find you need no calendar
to know it's November no more

The Last Day Of That Year

as I sail along December streets,
grease-hued slush splatters virgin snow
like regret belaboring hope
and I feel the coming of age-old age
in a way I never have

but my driving leaves me weary
of my usual Janu-wariness
and as my motor drones into the darkness
of those last remaining hours,
I can't say I'll be sorry
to put that year behind me finally

and, though the road
on rubber tires
me, and I'd like nothing
more than rest,
I won't welcome my next recline
amongst the death that lies
so close beside the sleep

Serving This Unpunctuated Sentence

in a dark and deafened room I sit
watching all I was and would have been
oozing oh so slowly out of me

and trickling down the table legs
to bleed into the rug
not four feet shy of bookshelves
cast in shades of afternoon

a wasted mass of protoplasm
sticking to the chair

music to my years

distilled song lyrics

And in the air above (and swirling all around) it all
have always been the songs: words bring meaning
to the music and music drives the words home.

A Color Undefined

I wish I were a color undefined;
a color yet to figure in,
so green and unfamiliar to their eyes

I wish I were a color still untried;
a color with no history,
no wavelength on the spectrum to belie;
a color all-encompassing
and swirling in the blackness and the white,
like melanin unblinded by the light

> yes, to break out of the black and white
> and join the colored people,
> intermingling our pigments
> 'til, too many to be labeled,
> we can't begin to think of one invalid,
> though unequaled,
> embracing every earnest shade –
> I wonder if we're able

I wish I were a color seen anew;
a color with no forefathers
to taint the reputation of my hue;
a color not foreshadowing
nor lending any clue
as to the differences
we'll find in me and you

> *repeat refrain*

As Long As I Can Run

been down on this bike, now
so damned many times
I'm surprised I still ride anymore

but as long as I can run
I fear I may run out of room
though I don't look for that
to happen soon

been down on these textbooks
so damned many times
I don't know what I know no more

but as long as I can think
I think I'll prob'ly think too much
which still somehow seems
nowhere near enough

> the new pain
> is really the old pain
> being felt on a whole 'nother plane
>
> the new world
> is really the old world
> with concrete poured over the ground
>
> and I got lost
> in the chorus
> while everyone else got so found

been down on my fathers
so damned many times
they've probably disowned me by now

but as long as I recall
it sets my head and heart to ache
and wishing we'd not make
the same mistakes

been down on these women
so damned many times
you'd think I'd have finally had my fill

but as long as I can dream
I'll prob'ly never get things done
and why would I just walk
if I could run

      the new pain
      is really the old pain
      being felt on a whole 'nother plane

      the new song's
      the same as the old song,
      new voices disguising the sound

      and I got lost
      in the chorus
      while everyone else got so found

As Stupid As I Feel

and on the first day
of my prime,
I set right out
to right the world –
all too sure that
these ideals
weren't gonna get lost
in the swirl

now years beyond those days have fallen
all across these fallow grounds –
if I was gonna get the calling,
I'd have gotten it by now

and my only consolation
as my images unreel
is that I probably don't look
anywhere near
as stupid as I feel
as stupid as I feel
as stupid as I feel

and on the last day
of the year,
I sat right down
to write the world –
all too swollen
with my problems
and all too long
gone un-girled

      now hope can surge half-hearted
      for a minute or an hour –
      if she wasn't gonna call me,
      I'm quite sure it would've been by now

      and my only consolation
      as the words and page congeal
      is that it probably won't sound
      anywhere near
      as stupid as it feels
      as stupid as it feels
      as stupid as it feels

Waiting For The Sky To Fall

beyond the laughter
of the foolish spring;
the bronzing skin
of pleasured summer:

I've watched the days
surpass the years
and felt these feelings
growin' number

       look outside, the clouds have gathered
       to do what clouds are bound to do –
       another day won't see me waiting
       for the sodden sky to fall all over you

and, come the dry eyes
of the sober fall;
the longed-for lips
of sullen winter:

you'll see the day
when all my swollen hopes
of you no longer
even glimmer

       go inside, the sky has fallen –
       now there's nothing left to be
       but half of what we could've hoped for
       with the paths of two entwining you and me

The Plot

from the first time that I saw you,
couldn't think of nothin' else –
how the world can overwhelm your
all-consuming sense of self;
thinking far into the future,
when the one and one are two:
it can't help but be too long
'til I'm lyin' next to you

you know that each time that I see you,
something's stickin' in my craw:
that no matter how we struggle,
we're, none of us, above the law(s) –
there's just no way to avoid it;
there's just nothing we can do:
it can't help but be too long
'til I'm lyin' next to you

since that last time that I saw you,
can't keep my mind on much at all
and even after all this time,
I can't bring myself to bear the pall –
ah, but all too soon I'm comforted
to realize anew:
it can't help but be too long
'til I'm lyin' next to you

Ouch

wherever there're winners,
there have to be losers –
it's just how the game is played;
wherever there's eating,
there have to be eaten –
that's the way this old world has been made;
as long as we're living, we're gonna keep dying
and loss only comes 'cause there's gain

    as long as you've already heard this before,
    it's hardly worth opening my mouth
    but as long as it keeps on hurting, my friend,
    the people will keep saying ouch

as long as suns come up,
suns have to go down –
I'm not the one writing the rules;
wherever belief is, there had to be doubt;
where warmth radiates, the source cools;
if you've finished building
what you hope to last,
you'd better hang on to your tools

    as much as we've been on this subject again,
    you'd think we'd have worn it all out
    but as long as it keeps on hurting,
    the people will keep saying ouch

as long as there's sex,
everyone's got to have it –
as long as they do, there'll be more;
as long as there's more,
there's bound to be less –
less room than the few had before;
as long as the burgeoning
squeezes the walls,
somebody will reach for the door

   as long as new doors are revealed, at length,
   there's some of us walking on out –
   'cause as long as it keeps on hurting the people,
   the people will keep saying ouch

The Days Of Here And Now

and on the verge of nothingness,
I made myself a vow:
that all the bloody screamingness
I've carried so deep down
would somehow spill out onto these,
the days of here and now

I swear it by my aching back,
the furrows of my brow:
the dead are as alive as all
the living will allow
in spite of all our dying in
the days of here and now

        death to the future
        and birth to the past,
        today's about as long
        as this living's gonna last
        and all the lies I've told myself
        to keep myself alive
        have grown so much less likely
        than biblically contrived

though I know what and where and when,
I still don't quite know how
or why it's even come to this –
I swear that right out loud:
I'm scrambling to take stock of these,
the days of here and now

attended by the lonely drone
of engines fueled by doubt,
a bilgeful of regret, forebodings
off the starboard bow,
I steam the naked, nervous, numbered
days of here and now

      none know what's coming,
      we all know what's gone –
      the question still remains,
      "is there life beneath the lawn?"
      and all the research shows the things
      the research hasn't shown,
      though we try to console ourselves
      each soul goes home alone

Whoa

whoa is me,
whoa is you,
whoa is when the whole wide world
got nothin' better to do
than to pull its reins on you

and I'm so full of whoa,
I can't even giddy-up no mo'

Lord, just a mule and forty acres –
that's all I ever asked of you;
well, this hard livin's made me so damned stubborn,
now I ain't gonna need that mule

'cause I'm so full of whoa,
I can't even giddy-up no mo'

now you can put me out to pasture –
you can strap me to the plow;
you can crack your whip across me
and I'll heave against the ground

but I'm so full of whoa,
I can't even giddy-up no mo

everybody say, "hold your horses!"
but I been holdin' them so long,
I can't help but feelin' somehow
that it's doin' me some wrong
(if'n you get my meanin')

      yeah,
      whoa is me,
      whoa is you,
      whoa is when the whole wide world
      got nothin' better to do
      than to pull its reins on you

      and I'm so full of whoa,
      I can't even giddy-up no mo'

If I Needed Something

when I was much more youthsome,
well, I used to drive a stick –
a carrot tied to one end,
let me tell you, I was quick

at cueing up the future
and then sizing up the work –
I leaned into my labors,
perspiration skunked my shirt

> I used to shrug it off like Sunday
> and the papers on the porch,
> from job to job and class to class, you
> know the sleeping spells were short

> and if I needed anything, it
> was a chance to earn my keep
> and a few hours to myself as
> yet another day went deep

> *instrumental break: fast forward forty years*

now lots of talk goes tongueless
when tomorrow is today,
though somehow history's still rewritten
when today is yesterday

but what was gonna matter
would've mattered long ago
and anything worth knowin',
well, by now we should've known

       I got no cause to get excited,
       now, I'm easily pessimized
       and as the cost outstrips the wages,
       I grow less and less surprised

       and if I still need anything,
       it's simply unencumbered sleep
       so I can wake to face the work
       of yet another waxing weak

Happy Is The Hardest Thing

one day you're six years on the job,
next day you're headin' back to school,
come summer, tradin' your tuition
for those monthly union dues

some time you're stuck in some same town
makin' a living with your tools,
too soon to find your wheels enrolled
in those old "grass is greener" blues

       for all the tossin' and the turnin'
       and the twistin' of these roads,
       can't find a place that's ripe for restin'
       or for layin' down this load

       the sun is sinkin', I'm just thinkin'
       with a drink in front of me:
       it seems like happy is the hardest
       thing I've ever tried to be

some folks, they tell me straightaway
I've got no right to be depressed –
that this behavior's unbecoming
of a life that's been so blessed

but I been workin', I been thinkin' –
I been feelin' sorry, too
an' I been figurin' a way
to try to make it up to you

> 'til it's okay for everybody,
> it's not gonna be okay
> and, though I don't know what to do 'bout
> that, it plagues me every day
>
> who's gonna tell you what you know
> too well, or else just don't believe –
> I tell ya, happy is the hardest
> thing you'll ever try to be

Hope On The Horizon

and back in the 18:00s;
the sun-weary sixes o'clock,
there wasn't much left
of the day or the life
to fuel my own flickering light

I lifted my head from my body,
gone leaden the length of the couch;
the shadows had slowly
enswallowed the room;
it seemed a long way to my feet

       there's hope on the horizon
       and I'm grasping for the thread;
       one minute I'll be dying
       and the next one I'll be dead

and back in the powder-blue darkness,
my eyes still trespass on the moon;
the same moon that's shone
on each present exchanged
for the mem'ries of long-greener pasts

I walk the deadly grey morning;
I can see what I've already seen,
my head so far above the cold earth,
it seems a long way to my feet

> "there's hope on the horizon",
> said the carrot to the stick,
> "a little faster and we'll be there",
> may just be life's cruelest trick

> "there's hope on the horizon",
> I was gasping for my breath;
> one minute I was dying
> and the next one I was dead

Appendix A: A chronology of these poems.

1987 (4 poems)

East Or Sunday[1]	06 Jan
Something #1	06 Apr
Just A Sky Away[4]	22 Oct
Reptime	03 Nov

1988 (8 poems)

Statistically Insignificant	11 Feb
Eight Mile Sigh	26 Feb
Full Cycle	27 Feb
Animals And Words	13 Mar
April, Come What May	22 Mar
Parting	29 Apr
Time-And-A-Half	11 Jul
Suburban Purpose	30 Nov

1989 (1 poem)

A Color Undefined[2]	12 May

1990 (3 poems)

Ouch[2]	23 Apr
Drinkin' Michigan	07 Aug
Whisperless	25 Aug

1991 (2 poems)

As Long As I Can Run[2]	06 Jan
Hope On The Horizon[2]	15 Jan

1992 (2 poems)

The Burning Leaves	05 Oct
Only For The Winter	23 Dec

1994 (2 poems)

Antarchitecture	19 Aug
A Bullet For The Future[1]	22 Sep

1995 (2 poems)

The Last Day Of That Year	31 Dec
At My Age	31 Dec

1996 (2 poems)

A Number One Than Yesterday	01 Jan
And In The Wake Of Sleep	06 Dec

1997 (4 poems)

Pard-on	23 Apr
Movement 101	13 Sep
Simple	04 Oct
Tissues In Eternity	09 Nov

1998 (1 poem)

Another Friday At 1900	07 Feb

1999 (2 poems)

Chromonymous	19 Aug
Down Fall	27 Oct

2000 (2 poems)

Midnight, Thirty-Eighth	08 May
Lasting	26 Jul

2002 (1 poem)

Ash Wednesday, A. D. 2002	26 Feb

2003 (2 poems)

Whoa[2]	04 Jan
Waiting For The Sky To Fall[2]	02 Nov

2004 (2 poems)

Pictures Of Life	09 Nov
As Stupid As I Feel[2]	31 Dec

2005 (1 poem)
The Plot[2]   25 Jun

2006 (1 poem)
This Shit   02 Dec

2009 (2 poems)
Vangi's House   17 May
And None For The Days Of Not   23 May

2012 (3 poems)
The Days Of Here And Now[3]   27 May
Far Things   28 Jul
I Walk The World   14 Oct

2013 (1 poem)
No Matter The Mercury   09 Dec

2016 (12 poems)
Serving This Unpunctuated Sentence   12 Jan
Happy Is The Hardest Thing[3]   23 Feb
If I Needed Something[3]   06 Apr
Eternitude[5]   04 Jul
Breverence   28 Jul
Stolen Moments Of Gladness #3   23 Aug
Slopeshot #99   30 Aug
On Sadder Day Mournings   31 Aug
Before The Fall   12 Sep
Who Would Want To Be The Last?   23 Oct
November No More   04 Nov
Six Feet   12 Nov

2017 (4 poems)
Zenadirith[6]   18 Jan
Some Assumptions   07 Apr
Brontitude   07 Sep
You Are Here   13 Nov

2018 (5 poems)

Vertebrates Of The United States[7]	04 Jan
From Here To Uncertainty	07 Apr
You're Still The You Of Your Youth	26 Apr
Contemperature	05 Jun
Under The Melanosphere	05 Jun

2019 (8 poems)

Dirt For Dessert	20 Jan
Sometimes I Lie So Wide	16 Apr
Writhing Scientific	05 Sep
The Earthen Autumnation	11 Oct
In The Lateness Of The Day	23 Oct
The End Of Almost Any Poem You'll Write	29 Oct
Groundless	30 Oct
Field Trip	31 Oct

37 of the poems from 1987 through 2013 (those not designated as song lyrics) were included in Tales From The Otherground (2014).

19 of the poems from 2016 through 2018 (those not designated as song lyrics) were included in Can't Forget The Motor City... (2018).

The 8 poems from 2019 have not been included in any previous Mag Pie collection.

1One of two old poems that haven't been included in recent collections.

2A song lyric: Visit josephnicks.com to hear the entire song as recorded by The Grist Minstrels in 2004 (6 songs + 2 unreleased demoes from 2005).

3One of three as-yet unrecorded song lyrics that are in need of music.

4previously published in Spectrum 10 (2017)
5previously published in Altadena Poetry Review (Anthology 2018)
6previously published in Spectrum 9 (2017)
7previously published in Spectrum 14 (2018)

Appendix B: Some historic works of boomslang worth researching.

Muscular Memoirs	Sarah Bellum
Drawn And Quartered Miles	Izzy Quikenov
Return to Granny Smith's Orchard	Annapola Dey
The 1970s: Decade Of Decay	Pete Humus
Ventriculist	Cora Soan
California Legless	Annie Ella Pulchra
Seventy-Eight Percent Nitrogen	Jocelyn Ferrer
Of Baculum And Tusk	Gugu Gajube
Gagging On Humanity	Kay Osko
The Unfulfilled Promise of Nature Unnurtured	Dee Ennay
What Is This Thing Called, Love?	Juana Petit
Rome Didn't Fall In A Day	Tim Burr

about the author

Since 1979, Detroit-born Joseph Nicks has divided his waking hours more-or-less equally between his "day job" and his nocturnal writing. The diurnal component has varied from manual laborer to water quality lab technician, assistant science advisor to a museum exhibits development team, technical writer, public school biology teacher, and field biologist.

He holds a B.S. in terrestrial zoology and two teaching credentials (multiple subject and biological sciences) and currently resides in the rural Mojave Desert. Recent publications include *Tales From The Otherground* (2014), *Songs From The Dirt* (2015), and *Can't Forget The Motor City...* (2018).

CPSIA information can be obtained
at www.ICGtesting.com
Printed in the USA
LVHW110838121020
668566LV00001B/180

9 780997 125795